102 Things to Do Before You Are Due

"Everybody leave me alone. I've had a busy day being pregnant and need to do it again tomorrow."

—Anonymous

102 THINGS TO DO BEFORE YOU ARE DUE

Dawn Dais

Art by Leticia Plate

duopress

INTRODUCTION

"Nine months is forever, then it's no time at all."

—Parent of four children

When I went into labor a week early with our first baby, my partner immediately started hanging a ceiling fan in the nursery. We had heard that ceiling fans help circulate the air and therefore can reduce the chance of SIDS (sudden infant death syndrome). But we hadn't quite gotten around to installing the fan by week 39. So while I was having contractions in the master bedroom, there was a home improvement project going on in the nursery. Because we HAD TO GET ALL THE THINGS DONE BEFORE THE BABY ARRIVED! Don't mind that we were planning on keeping the baby in a bassinet next to our bed for the first few months. Rational thought has a tendency to be replaced by utter panic the second childbirth begins.

I love the quote at the top of this page because it perfectly sums up pregnancy: "Nine months is forever." Not "Nine months feels like forever." When you are in it, nine months is forever. You are growing a little speck of dust into something the size of an alarmingly large piece of fruit (or a fruit salad, if you are having multiples). Your body sloooowly expands to accommodate this new tenant, and the months can feel like years as you waddle your way through them.

But then you get to the finish line and all of a sudden it feels too soon. You need more time! You aren't ready! There are ceiling fans to install!

After you have your baby and the months turn into years, pregnancy begins to feel like no time at all. In the grand scheme of things, it's a tiny little blip (albeit one in which you feel more like a blimp).

This book is for the time when pregnancy is forever. When you're scared and excited, sure and clueless, ecstatic and prone to fits of rage cleaning. It's compact and easily digestible because pregnant ladies are tired and doing something easy is a welcome change when you've spent your days battling all-day morning sickness and/ or the inability to put your socks on without bringing in an assistant.

Early on in my parenting life I wrote a series of books called The Sh!t No One Tells You. They are about pregnancy, babies, toddlers, and various other highlights of procreation. My inspiration for these books came from the fact that at every turn along my childrearing road, I kept finding more and more sh!t no one had warned me about. I felt it my duty to share this sh!t with the world (we all have our callings in life, mine just happens to involve profanity [my parents are very proud]).

Once I started writing the books I also started hearing from other moms who related to what I had to say. We all love our children with every fiber of our being, but also, our fibers are tiiiired. We genuinely want to do the very best for our kids, but also, most days we feel like our parenting skills are hovering around a C- grade. We value our doctors and other professionals who are educated on all matters having to do with pregnancy and children, but also, we've come to cherish the opinions of fellow moms who have been educated at the Graduate School of Living with Tiny Humans.

So that's what you'll find in this book, a straightforward pregnancy strategy, from a fellow mom who has navigated her way through the production of two watermelons. These 102 tips are in no way an all-encompassing look into gestation, and all 102 aren't a prerequisite to completing pregnancy. Your baby is coming whether or not you do all of these things before you are due. But I do think these 102 tips will help you maximize your pregnancy months and send you into parenthood with a solid game plan.

My tips range from your registry, baby shower, and birth plan, to babymoons, career prep, and dealing with annoying people. Flip through this book and check some of these to-do's off your list. Use them as a jumping-off point to explore the topics that are most important to you. Combine them with other books, with plenty of trusted advice, and with your own natural instincts.

And maybe do all this before your contractions start. Trust me on that one.

Have fun with this book, and with your pregnancy. Enjoy these last few months before baby and allow yourself to get excited about the upcoming arrival of your new roommate. Before you know it he or she will be here, filling your life with spit-up, diapers, and more love than you ever imagined possible. Because pregnancy is forever, then it's no time at all.

CHAPTER 1

PEEING ON THE STICK

*Things to Do as Soon as You
Find Out You're Pregnant*

Whether your pregnancy was an *oopsie* or involved intricately charted ovulation cycles, you are most likely going to kick off this party with a home pregnancy test. Or ten. And there you'll be sitting, on the toilet or the bathroom floor, staring at a little stick, waiting for it to change your entire life.

If it gives you the positive sign, that bathroom becomes the beginning of your most important story.

But what do you do next?

1. FREAK OUT

As soon as the test screams out, "Lady, you're all the way preggers!" you'll have a lot of emotions. You may be ecstatic, terrified, shocked, or otherwise unable to move because there are too many thoughts racing through your brain all at the same time.

I say lean into that crazy for a little bit. Allow yourself to freak out and scream or cry or hyperventilate. This is big. There is no overreacting.

2. Take MORE TESTS

If you're like me, you'll probably need more than one test to confirm that this is really happening. I took at least five pregnancy tests the first day and continued to randomly test myself for months. In the beginning, before you are showing or feeling kicks, pregnancy tests are the best way to remind yourself that you are actually building a human (or two, or three!) inside your body.

3. Download a PREGNANCY APP

Another way to feel connected to your pregnancy (without spending tons of money on pregnancy tests) is to keep constant tabs on what is happening at different stages of your baby-making experiment. Apps (What to Expect Pregnancy App, Hello Belly, WebMD Pregnancy App, The Bump Pregnancy App to name just a few) provide week-by-week descriptions of your baby and your body, as well as helpful articles, interactive FAQs, and even baby-naming help. Apps can provide comfort and knowledge throughout your pregnancy, and having them right at your fingertips will prove priceless.

4: GET ALL THE PREGNANCY BOOKS

I'm not sure why pregnant women need to gather up every single pregnancy book ever written, but they do, so you should, too. There are books written strictly from a medical perspective and some written from a humorous or relatable perspective. But all of them are written so that you can pile them on your nightstand and constantly be in close proximity to pages and pages of pregnancy information. So go raid the bookstore or the library and pile away. Even if you don't actually read all the books cover to cover, there is something quite comforting about having them nearby.

Chapter 2

Go Team!

Tips on Keeping Your Partner Involved in the Journey

Pregnancy is only happening inside of one person's body, but that doesn't mean that partners can't get involved as well. Gestation is a really important time in both parents' lives, but sometimes partners can feel hesitant to stake their claim to the process. Help your partner feel more connected to the baby and your pregnancy by getting them involved in every step.

Keep in mind that some partners might need a little guidance in this area. A lot of partners want to help but just aren't sure exactly how. So don't wait for your partner to do the things you want them to do to support your pregnancy—tell them what you want. Be clear and concise. They aren't children that need to be spoken down to, but they also aren't mind readers. Delegate, articulate, and reiterate.

5. GO TO PRENATAL APPOINTMENTS TOGETHER

Pregnancy involves a lot of unknowns, which can be scary and confusing for both partners. The best place to find answers to those unknowns is at your prenatal appointments. Having both partners at prenatal appointments is a great way for expectant parents to ask questions and learn more about what is happening inside the Baby Mama. (WARNING: What's happening inside [and how it intends to get outside] of Baby Mama can be quite alarming to the uninitiated. You and your partner might want to take a quick skim through a couple of those pregnancy books before the first doctor's appointment, to build up your tolerance for placenta talk well in advance.)

Doctor's appointments also offer ultrasounds and heartbeat monitoring, which are two ways to instantly melt an expectant parent's heart. Babies have a way of becoming very real the second you hear that heartbeat or see that little alien swimming around on the ultrasound monitor. These moments can really help your partner connect with the unborn baby, so try to plan your doctor appointments at times when both of you can attend.

6. Read Through Baby Name Books Together

Picking a name for your baby, the moniker they will carry for THEIR ENTIRE LIVES, is not an easy task. But it can be a fun one. Grab one of those 2,000-page books (or find a baby naming app) with every name ever uttered and start scouring for the perfect one. It may be months before you find a name you both actually like, but in the meantime there are hours of fun waiting for the two of you as you mercilessly mock 97% of the options.

1. PLAN TOGETHER

There are a lot of plans to be made regarding your baby. Keep your partner involved in all of these plans, from nursery decoration to medical and delivery choices. It's important to start off this parenting journey with the clear understanding that you two are in this together.

8. KEEP IN TOUCH

It can be difficult for a partner to feel connected to a pregnancy that is happening in another person's body. Encourage your partner to talk or sing to your baby/belly throughout your pregnancy. There is evidence to suggest that the baby will be listening and may even grow familiar with that voice by the time they pop out.

Once the baby starts kicking hard enough to be felt from the outside, share the experience with your partner. Their face will light up when you place their hand on your belly and they feel their baby kick hello for the first time. Alternatively, their face may light up in fear because 1) kicks mean this is really happening and 2) they've seen a lot of sci-fi movies where aliens kick their way out of torsos.

Chapter 3

PREGNANCY ANNOUNCEMENTS

When and How to Announce to All the Different People in Your Life

You're pregnant! This is big news! Normally you would want to share big news with the world, but pregnancy news apparently has to be doled out on a schedule. It's a rule. Written by whom, I do not know.

In this chapter I give tips on how to tell the world about your good news, but keep in mind that this is a very personal choice and a bell you can't unring once you've made the announcement. So never rush your announcement if you aren't ready. The world will understand.

9. ANNOUNCE TO CLOSE FRIENDS AND FAMILY

The general rule for pregnancy announcements is that they should be made after week 12, or after the first trimester. The thought is that the chances of miscarrying go down after the first trimester, and no one wants to make a happy announcement that is later followed up by a very sad one.

As I mentioned previously, deciding when to announce your pregnancy is a deeply personal choice. In my case I chose to tell very close family and friends as soon as the pregnancy test gave me a positive sign. My thinking was that even if I did miscarry I would want these people to know that news as well.

The announcement of pregnancy to close friends and family has taken on a life of its own the past few years. According to the internet and social media, a simple phone call is no longer sufficient. These days grandparents need to be alerted via elaborate games of charades, and choreography and confetti are required when telling friends. I wouldn't be surprised if someone somewhere has enlisted the help of an actual stork in their announcement production.

I say go big with your announcement. Why not? This is exciting news! It deserves a little panache. Also, pregnancy marks the last time you are going to have the energy to dedicate to anything remotely elaborate, so you might as well maximize your last few months of organizational skills.

But then also, there's a chance you'll be tired and bloated and nauseous and not have the energy or inclination for panache. In that case I say ignore the internet's ridiculous pressures and just announce via phone call or perhaps a text, if your fingers are the only part of your body that is able to move.

10. ALERT YOUR FRIENDS

Alerting your friends about your pregnancy can seem like a daunting undertaking. You don't have time to call every single person, but you also don't want anyone to feel left out of this special news. I recommend putting together a text or email to friends after you've reached your second trimester. If you aren't ready for the announcement to be shared with the entire world, take the time to mention that you are keeping the news off of social media so that you aren't outed online before you are ready.

If you have any energy left over from your close friends and family announcement production try to put together a cute photo or video to share the news. The internet has a million and one announcement ideas, but my favorites have always involved little baby shoes, onesies with "Coming Soon" written on them, and any time "Ice, Ice, Baby" is incorporated. I'm a sucker for the classics.

11. Share at Work

Work can be a tricky place to announce you are pregnant. By law, a woman can't be fired or demoted for being pregnant, but that doesn't mean everyone has the luxury of feeling 100% confident in their employment during and after pregnancy. Your safety is the most important thing, so if your job requires physical activity that may put your pregnancy at risk, then you should tell your employer immediately. Other than that, it's really up to you when you feel comfortable sharing your news in the workplace.

If you are experiencing bad morning sickness you might want to at least give your boss a head's up as to why you are going to appear hungover for the foreseeable future (until the child is about 25 years old). Or, if you are feeling feisty you can play a game with coworkers wherein you see how big your belly can get before some brave/stupid soul dares to ask you if you are pregnant.

12. Tell The World

These days a baby is not official until its impending arrival has been shared via social media. When you are ready to let the entire world know that you are acting as an incubator for a tiny human(s), then social media is the place to play. Put some thought into this announcement. Think adorable/funny photos or videos, think props and puns and high production value. This is your child's introduction to the world! Go big.

13. Reveal The Gender

After you've announced your pregnancy to every person on the planet, your work in the revelation department is not done. These days it is mandated that you also let everyone on the entire planet know the gender of the child(ren) you are carrying. Gender reveal parties and announcements have taken on a life of their own the past few years, and you too might want to find out the gender of your child in a way that involves a party planner and pink or blue cake.

Some couples have their doctor write down the gender and put it in an envelope, then trust one lucky friend to bake a pink cake or load a big cardboard box with blue balloons. You can have a picture/video taken of the color reveal and share it with friends and family, or you can invite them all over for a huge party to learn the big news along with you. Another option is to host a party after you've learned the gender and use the color of party drinks or your outfit to let guests in on the secret.

14. PREPARE TO ANNOUNCE THE BABY

This might seem a little premature, but it's never a bad idea to get a jump on absolutely anything that can be checked off your to-do list before baby arrives. Go on a card-designing site like Shutterfly and pick out a birth announcement you like. Fill in whatever information you can, pick the colors you like, and put it safely in your Saved Projects file. Then, once you've given birth all you have to do is take a few pictures, fill in a few stats, and hit order. Future you will be glad you set everything up for her success.

Chapter 4

YOUR DOCTOR

*Tips on Picking a Doctor for
This Wild Ride*

Your obstetrician will be with you on your journey toward parenthood. In fact they will be the one making sure everything goes well along the way. It's important that you find a doctor you trust and one who will respect your wishes when it comes to your baby in utero and during delivery.

Check with your insurance first to find out which doctors are available with your coverage. Then look them up online to see what reviews have been left about them. Doing your homework will help you narrow down the list of potential doctors and allow you the best chance of connecting with the right one from the beginning.

15. ASK FAMILY AND FRIENDS FOR RECOMMENDATIONS

Getting a recommendation from a friend or family member is a great way to start your obstetrician search. Be sure to limit your advice request to friends and family who you know had similar birth plans to yours and generally hold the same philosophies regarding pregnancy and childbirth. For instance, if your best friend had a silent birth in her living room and you are planning on giving birth with the help of an epidural and cuss words, you might want to skip her recommendation.

16. VISIT a COUPLE OF DOCTORS

Take the time to meet with a few doctors before making your final decision. Get a feel for their pregnancy and delivery philosophies by asking roughly 800 questions. These questions will have a lot to do with your own personal desires for your pregnancy and the birth of your child. Are you wanting to go all natural? Involve a midwife or a doula? How do you feel about induction or monitoring during delivery? Are you concerned about having to get a C-section? An episiotomy? Jot down all of these questions and concerns and discuss them with your potential doctor. Your goal is to find an obstetrician who supports your birth plan and will help you successfully execute that plan. It's also a good idea to pick a doctor who is unfazed by incessant questioning right from the beginning since your prenatal appointments are going to consist mainly of you bringing in a list of 400 things you are worried about each time you visit.

Also keep in mind that there is a chance your doctor won't be available when you go into labor, as babies are not big on making their arrivals at convenient times. Ask your potential doctor about the backup obstetricians that may become your deliver doctor. Do they meet all of your qualifications as well?

17. THEIR DELIVERY HOSPITAL

A doctor's delivery hospital is one of the biggest things to consider when making your choice. Visit their delivery hospital and make sure it meets your expectations. Proximity to your house is one factor to consider when evaluating a hospital, since you'll want to be close by in the case of an emergency or quick delivery scenario. But more importantly, does the hospital have a neonatal intensive care unit (NICU) that provides care for extremely premature or critically ill newborns? I personally picked a hospital that was farther away from my house, simply because it had a NICU. This provided me a peace of mind that was worth a little longer drive.

Midwife vs. Doula

A midwife is a licensed medical professional. Depending on where the midwife practices they can usually perform prenatal exams as well as write prescriptions and monitor the baby in utero. Midwives usually focus on limiting technological interventions during pregnancy, but they are trained to refer a pregnant woman to an obstetrician if complications arise outside of their ability to manage. They are trained and qualified to deliver (catch) babies.

Doulas are cheerleaders of sorts. They are there to help you develop a birth plan and then offer you support throughout your delivery. If you are interested in having a doula you should start looking for one in your second trimester and interview several before making your choice. Maybe take them each to Costco on a Saturday afternoon to see how the two of you navigate stressful situations together.

CHAPTER 5

The Baby's Doctor

Tips for Picking a Pediatrician

Picking a doctor for your baby is a big decision. It can be really comforting to link up with a good pediatrician from the beginning of your child's life. They will get to know your child and become a partner in your baby's health. Do your research and make some office visits before the baby arrives. Start your search around week 30 of your pregnancy, giving you plenty of time to pick the right doctor before the baby is born.

18. ASK FAMILY and FRIENDS FOR RECOMMENDATIONS

Friends and family with kids should always be your first stop when you are in need of recommendations for anything having to do with your baby. They are like your own personal Yelp. Ask your network for pediatricians they trust (and what they like about their doctor) and add those names to your list of possibilities.

19. USE THE INTERNET

The internet is a great place to do some intense research. Go to *Healthychildren.org -> Tips and Tools -> Find a Pediatrician* to search for American Academy of Pediatrics doctors in your area (or Caringforkids.cps.ca for Canadian pediatricians). Mom groups on social media are also a great resource when searching for a doctor. Moms are always ready (sometimes a little too ready) to give their opinions (and warnings) and won't hesitate to share their experiences with different doctors in your area.

20. MAP OUT THE DISTANCE

Once you have a baby, convenience will play a very large role in all of your decisions. When you've narrowed down your list of potential pediatricians, grab the baby stroller and do a dry run to each potential office (maybe throw some blankets and a doll in the stroller so you don't look completely insane during this pre-baby exercise). The closest office with the best parking should move very far up the list immediately. If you are in a big city and reliant on public transportation, this dry run can be even more important. What offices are near subway stations? What stations have elevators? What is the least traumatizing route between your home and a medical professional? Pick that one.

21. SET AN APPOINTMENT

Sometimes you just need to get face-to-face with a doctor to really decide if they are right for you. Set up introduction appointments with a few potential pediatricians and bring a list of important questions to ask. Find out each doctor's opinions on matters such as vaccinations, sleep training, breastfeeding, and circumcision. Try to gauge how uptight they are because you're going to want a doctor who goes with the flow and keeps you calm when you are freaking out about every little hiccup your new baby has.

Find out their office hours and how emergencies are handled when the office is closed. With a new baby you will often have a lot of questions, so ask if the doctor is available for phone appointments and email correspondence. Also, find out their policy on same day appointments if needed.

Take a look around the office and chat with the staff; get a feeling for the way they do business and decide if it feels like a good fit.

Chapter 6

JOURNAL IT

*Tips on Ways to Capture Your
Pregnancy Journey for Posterity*

It's hard to wrap your mind around what is coming your way—how your life is going to change with the arrival of your child. When you're in it, pregnancy can seem like a long trudge up a hill covered in hormones and stretchy pants. But upon reflection it will take on a different appearance. Years from now you'll look back on pregnancy as the beginning of something new. A new version of you, really. (A version that stays covered in hormones and stretchy pants, coincidentally.)

Take the time to document these last few months before you officially move over to the parenting portion of your life. It will be fun to look back on this time and remember what you looked like, how you were feeling, and how innocent you still were.

22. POST TO SOCIAL MEDIA

Share your pregnancy highlights via social media, getting you and your virtual buddies ready for the inundation of baby photos and tidbits that are just around the bend. Assign a hashtag for your baby so that you can easily find all your pregnancy- and baby-related posts in a pinch. There are online resources (like Mysocialbook.com) that allow you to print out your social media feeds into bound books. Keep that in mind and post often during your pregnancy so that you can easily print out your pregnancy months into a book that documents your journey.

23. KEEP a JOURNaL/PhOTO AlbUM

Get crazy and keep a real live journal during your pregnancy. Chart your gestation with quick entries about your pregnancy experience. Write letters to your baby telling them how much you are thinking about them, how much you are planning for them, how much you want to provide for them. Get deep. Include pictures and ultrasound images and anything else that documents these months. This may seem like a lot of work, but it's going to be a long while before you have the time or inclination to do something of this nature again: Parenthood tends to put the brakes on introspection and crafting. So grab your pen and your glue stick and start making a scrapbook/journal combination that will dazzle.

Chapter 7

NUTRITION and EXERCISE

What to Eat, How to Move

I have some bad news. "Eating for two" doesn't mean pregnant women get to binge eat snacks for 9 months straight. I know, it's a bummer. Weight gain is a natural part of pregnancy, but it's recommended that you eat only 300 extra calories per day, and that increase isn't even advised until your second and third trimesters of pregnancy.

While indulging in the occasional craving is not against the rules, it's always a good idea to practice healthy habits from the beginning of your pregnancy. Here are some tips on how to do that.

24. Be a Balanced Rainbow

If you have morning sickness (or all-day sickness like I did) then your priority is eating whatever foods don't upset your protesting belly. But as soon as you are able, it's important to implement a balanced diet. Eat a rainbow of foods (fruits, veggies, yogurts, nuts, meat, eggs, etc.) and try to get as many vitamins as you can (complement your rainbow with a prenatal vitamin and an iron supplement as well). Try to not overdo it on carbs, as they spike your blood glucose levels and might increase your chances of gestational diabetes.

Also, eating several small meals throughout the day is a great way to keep your body enriched and can even help when you are still battling morning sickness. Wash down your rainbow with plenty of water, as hydration is very important during pregnancy.

25. KEEP MOVING

As you get bigger and bigger you are going to be less and less interested in moving your expanding body in any direction that isn't toward a recliner. But for the sake of your baby and your body, try to get up and move as much as you can throughout your pregnancy. Even maintaining a regular walking habit during your gestation will help keep you healthy and may even make your delivery a little easier.

If you worked out a lot before you got pregnant ask your doctor about safe ways to maintain your active lifestyle. Often it will be okay to continue working out—you'll just need to listen to your body and not push it past its new comfort zone.

26. BE SAFE

Before taking on any exercise regiment or sampling new food, always pause and remember that you have a passenger onboard who is counting on you. Don't overexert yourself physically or eat foods that have been deemed unsafe for pregnant women (raw foods, deli meat, unpasteurized dairy products, booze). When in doubt, err on the side of caution and resign yourself to the fact that you will be sushi- and cookie dough-free for the foreseeable future. I know, it's hard. But you can do it.

21. SPLURGE

Look, it's important to eat a healthy, balanced diet. And it's important to move your body throughout your pregnancy. We all know this. We all strive for this. But listen, sometimes you just gotta splurge a little. Sometimes you have to lean into the fact that you are HUNGRY and TIRED. Why not combine those two feelings with an amazing afternoon spent on the couch napping and snacking on whatever food you want because you are building a human from scratch and you deserve a treat.

Chapter 8

CONTROL YOUR URGE TO BUY ALL THE THINGS

How to Keep Your Hormones from Having Access to Your Credit Cards

Once you find out you are pregnant something switches on in your brain. The wave of pregnancy hormones somehow hits a "Buy" button and you suddenly have the overwhelming urge to BUY ALL THE THINGS. Maybe it's a form of nesting, maybe you are just excited, but whatever it is, it ain't cheap.

Corporations throughout the land are very aware of pregnant mothers' need to spend money, and they are here to help. There are countless huge stores available to provide these pregnant ladies with a place to follow their natural purchasing instincts. These stores are expansive and can get very expensive. Here are some tips on how to make it through pregnancy without spending a fortune.

28. Proceed with Caution

Understand that you are in a weak state, and proceed with caution when you enter any store that features any sort of baby items. You do not need everything in the store. Your baby does not need everything in the store. I know that all the items are bright and shiny and new and promise to make you a certified parenting pro upon purchase. But you must be strong!

Most baby items can be found for cheap or free at secondhand stores or via bags of hand-me-downs from friends. Babies use baby items for approximately 14 seconds before getting bored with and/or outgrowing them. Try to remember this before you convince yourself that you need to spend thousands of dollars on shiny new baby doodads.

If you have friends with kids think about starting a hand-me-down network wherein you pass baby stuff around to each other instead of shopping with abandon. If you don't have friends with kids I highly recommend you find some. Go to the park and strike up conversations with moms that have one- or two-year-old children. Get on their good side (think coffee and pastries) and then casually ask them to give you all of their child's clothing when they are done with it.

29. START a PINTEREST BOARD

Shopping is fun, I get it. You are excited about your impending arrival and want to buy all the things so that you are prepared. But big stores and internet shops can be overwhelming in their amplitude. So before you start swiping that credit card, do a little planning.

Head to Pinterest and start a few baby boards (Baby Clothes, Baby Nursery, Baby Items, Mommy Needs All This Stuff). Scour the web for ideas and opinions, then add your favorites to your boards. After that you will probably have roughly 694 items posted. Maybe keep the credit card locked up until you get it whittled down a bit more.

30. START YOUR REGISTRY EARLY

Another way to fend off your spending urges is to start your registry list early so that other people can spend for you! This might seem silly, but there's no reason you can't start building your registry list early on, then add and subtract items as your baby shower date approaches.

Ask your friends with kids what they recommend putting on your registry, look online for registry tips, and pick one or two places to register. It's a good idea to register at more than one store, to provide purchasing options for friends and family who are looking for ordering ease when buying you a gift. The website Thebump.com/registry offers a place to consolidate your registries, with one handy link and a phone app to access everything.

31. FiNd The FRee STuFf

There are a lot of free or pretty cheap baby items available if you're willing to join some email lists or do a little internet searching. If you search "Free Baby Products," you'll find companies offering free samples of their baby products (diapers/formula/bottles/wipes/etc.). Or type in "Free Baby Items Just Pay Shipping" in your browser's search bar and let the internet guide you toward "almost free" items. As made obvious by the search term, most of these items require you to pay (high) shipping costs, but you can usually find a good deal or two among the available items. My favorites were the car seat and breastfeeding covers I got off of these sites.

32. SPLURGE a LITTLE

Yes, we want to keep our pregnancy spending under control. And raging hormones are not a valid reason for racking up crazy credit card debt. But also, you're pregnant! With a baby! That's exciting! Allow yourself a little splurge to celebrate. Pick up some adorable onesies or maybe some baby shoes that are the cutest (and most unnecessary) things you've ever seen. Buying a few baby items can help make your pregnancy feel real before you actually start feeling anything happening in your body.

EXTRA: REGISTRY LIST

- [ ] 20 onesies (no buttons or snaps! Newborn and infant sizes)
- [ ] 20 bibs (Babies drool. A lot.)
- [ ] Soft no-scratch baby mittens
- [ ] Baby monitor
- [ ] Cool mist humidifier
- [ ] Baby bathtub
- [ ] 2 diaper pails (for different parts of the house)
- [ ] 2–3 changing pads/5 changing pad covers (ready for poop at all times)
- [ ] Whole bunch of diapers (not just newborn—they'll grow out of those quickly)
- [ ] Diaper cream
- [ ] Unscented, sensitive-skin butt wipes
- [ ] Baby thermometer (head and ear)
- [ ] Pacifiers (the ones that have a little animal attached)
- [ ] Crib mattress protector x 2 (for middle-of-the-night quick changes)
- [ ] Baby breathing monitor (for peace of mind)
- [ ] 1 car seat
- [ ] Car seat bases to put in all your cars
- [ ] 10 bottles (buy different kinds—who knows what your kid will like)
- [ ] Bottle brush
- [ ] Bottle drying rack
- [ ] Breast pump
- [ ] Milk storage bags
- [ ] Nursing pillow

ChAPTER 9

HOW TO DeAl WiTh ANNOYiNG PEOPle

Tips on Dealing with the Public at Large, as You Grow Larger

For some reason everyone on the planet seems to have an opinion regarding pregnancy, and for some other reason all those people feel like it's okay to share their opinions with every pregnant woman they encounter. Apparently procreation brings out the annoying in people, so in this chapter we cover how to deal with these people and their annoying ways.

33. Nosey Nelly

Nosey Nelly is the person (sometimes a friend, but most of the time a complete stranger) who needs to get all up in the business of any and all pregnant women. They want to know about the gender, your birth plan, how many kids you want to have, if you plan to breastfeed, and if you had fertility issues. They can't stop asking questions. The best way to deal with these people is to simply not answer the questions. If you answer one you'll be stuck answering 500, so cut it off at the pass by giving them an "I don't know" and quickly transition into asking them a series of intrusive questions.

34. Chatty Cathy

Cathy knows things, she's intuitive, she's had life experiences, and she's read a whole lot of articles on the internet. She's practically a doctor, minus, you know, the education. Cathy needs to tell you all the things she knows because it is her job to keep others as informed as she is. Whatever Cathy says, just go with it. Give her a nod and a smile and agree. She thinks that the child will be born early because Mercury is in retrograde? "Me too, Cathy, I totally agree." Life is too short to engage with Cathy in any way that may prolong your conversation.

35. TOUChY TiNa

Touchy Tina can't keep her hands off of your pregnant belly. She just can't. Your belly is pushed way out into the world, and Tina treats it like a hand extended for a handshake. When I was pregnant I just let people touch my belly because I wasn't brave enough to tell them to stop and I didn't want things to get awkward. But it's your belly and your decision. If you don't want touching from Tina, you could always try this as she's swooping in: "You know, I've developed the weirdest rash on my belly. The doctor has no idea where it came from but thinks it can spread pretty easily!"

36. Panicked Pam

Pam is just like Cathy in that she's read a lot of internet articles. Unlike Cathy, the internet has sent Pam into a constant state of panic because she's only read the articles about scary medical occurrences. Pam is panicked and wants you to know about all the things that can go wrong during pregnancy and childbirth because you need to be panicked just like her. Try the nod-and-smile approach with Pam and hope that her information dump doesn't last too long. And then, whatever you do, DON'T RUN TO THE INTERNET AND LOOK UP ANYTHING PAM TOLD YOU. Or you will end up a Panicked Preggers.

37. The Old Wife

Without fail your pregnancy will bring out the sharing of every old wives' tale ever uttered throughout the globe. If you have heartburn, your baby will have a lot of hair; if you look at an animal for too long your baby will come out looking like that animal; if you are carrying high you are having a girl; if you smell like garlic you are having a boy; keep a knife under your bed to ward off evil spirits; stay away from cemeteries because the spirits hang out there, too; if you see an eclipse your baby will have a harelip; and so on, and so on and on and on. I personally find all of these superstitions endlessly entertaining, so I recommend grabbing some popcorn and settling in for some stories when you come across an Old Wife. Also, a knife under your bed isn't a horrible idea...

Chapter 10

The Side Effects

How to Deal with All the Fun
That Pregnancy Wreaks on Your Body

I always like to think of pregnancy as the ultimate science experiment. And with the number of side effects that come along with gestation it seems as though it's one of those science experiments where a lot of things are exploding or boiling over to make a big mess all over the laboratory. From hemorrhoids to heartburn, and bloody gums to varicose veins, pregnancy has fun written all over it. Here are some ways to roll with the punches your body is taking for the sake of procreation.

38. Fight the Feelings

Morning (really all-day) sickness is one of the worst side effects of pregnancy. It can last for months and months with little to no options for complete relief. If you are battling nausea I recommend stockpiling crackers, hard candies, ginger candies, and Sea-Bands (these are wristbands that hit a pressure point that can help with seasickness and perhaps pregnancy sickness, too). Try any and all options for helping ease your pain, but also be gentle with yourself and rest as much as you can. Sometimes pulling the covers over your head and disappearing into sleep is the only way to alleviate pregnancy nausea, so try to indulge in a siesta whenever possible.

39. Accept Your Crazy

Pregnancy hormones and the emotions they bring about are nothing to be trifled with. Let this be a warning to you and everyone in your general vicinity. No one wants to feel like they are imbalanced, but it's not a bad idea to accept early and often that pregnancy makes you a bit looney tunes. One minute you are laughing, the next you're crying, and the next you are very, very angry for reasons that make very, very little sense. Your spawn has hijacked your emotions and has no intention of returning them to their original location anytime soon. Try to keep this in mind as you feel yourself spinning off into a tantrum, and once you stop spinning be sure to apologize to any and all innocent bystanders.

40. Make a List

The fact is, pregnancy brings a lot of funky side effects along with it, and most of them will have little to no solution besides time and continuous complaining. But it's never a bad idea to keep a list of any side effects you are experiencing. Share that list with your doctor at your prenatal appointments just in case one of your side effects is a sign of something more serious (for instance severe itchiness can be a warning sign of cholestasis, which is a treatable but potentially harmful condition).

Chapter 11

LET'S GET COMFY

Clothing, Pillows, and Other Items a Preggo Woman Needs to Feel Human

It turns out that growing a watermelon in your uterus can be a less-than-comfortable undertaking. Spoiler alert. During pregnancy it seems as though everything on your body is getting bigger just as your energy levels take a nosedive. It's not the best combination.

The good news is that product manufacturers have heard the cries (and a lot of cussing as well) of pregnant women and now offer a multitude of items to help ease the pain of watermelon production. A lot of these products are not cheap, and it may seem silly to spend so much money on something that will only be used for a matter of months. But trust me when I tell you that your pregnancy comfort is worth the cost.

41. GET a PREGNANCY PillOW

When I was pregnant my nightly comfort ritual became a complex two-man assembly job. There were pillows everywhere. Under my head, under my belly, between my legs, and pushed up along the length of my back. Perhaps I should have done a little research into pregnancy pillows and cut a half hour of prep time off my nighttime routine.

The pregnancy pillow options are diverse and plentiful. For side sleepers there are U-shaped pillows that engulf you in a comfortable hug. For back sleepers the U becomes almost an O. For stomach sleepers there are blow-up beds with belly holes. If all of this sounds a bit cumbersome there are also pregnancy wedge pillows that are tiny and can be wedged under your belly, between your legs, or along your back.

Sleep becomes increasingly illusive the bigger your baby bump gets, so I recommend buying all the pregnancy pillows, piling them on your bed, and hoping they will bless you with extended shut-eye.

42. EVOLVE FROM WAIST EXTENDERS TO BELLY BANDS TO ELASTIC PANTS

During a woman's first pregnancy, she will often fight the transition to maternity pants. Maybe she doesn't want to spend the money on maternity clothes, maybe she doesn't want to lose her wardrobe for the duration of her pregnancy, maybe she is not giving up without a fight against physics and her expanding waistline.

Whatever her reasons there are waist extenders available to keep stubborn pregnant women in their non-maternity wear for as long as scientifically possible. A waist extender is a piece of elastic that has a button on one end and a button hole on the other. It allows the wearer to pop open tight pants and add a few extra inches to the waist. As the belly gets bigger and bigger and the pants' zipper loses its fight to stay up, waist extenders can be combined with fabric panels that are tucked into pants to keep underwear under wraps. This is not a great look overall, so you are going to want to combine all of this with a baggie shirt that covers up the belly breaking free of your pants.

Another option for extending the usability of your non-maternity wear is belly bands. These stretchy bands are worn from beneath the waistline up to the belly, covering unbuttoned pants and holding everything in place.

At some point maternity pants will become part of the wardrobe, and when they do it may be years before they leave again. I mean, who can argue with the comfort and convenience of elastic waistlines? Pregnancy leggings are also a good addition since they are stretchy all the time and will be comfortable post-baby as well.

43. EMBRACE THE BIG-ASS BRA

Along with everything else, boobs have a tendency to get big during the pregnancy months. Get the girls some proper support via a big-ass bra. Your back will thank you for it. Fight the instinct to buy a big-ass nursing bra while you are pregnant because your boobs are most likely going to change in size after you give birth.

44. Add Some Maternity Tank Tops

Maternity tank tops are comfy, and some are built with features that support your boobs, back, and belly, making them extra fun. They can also be worn for months (years?) after the baby arrives, giving them added value.

45. Buy Some Comfortable Shoes

Women have a tendency to love shoes. And those shoes have a tendency to be more focused on fashion than comfort. During pregnancy it might be time to let go of fashion for a few months. For the sake of your joints, muscles, and sanity, grab a couple pairs of shoes that will support you during your progression toward waddling. Think comfort, think slip-on, think a size too big (your belly isn't the only thing that is going to expand).

Chapter 12

It's Time to Adult

*Tips on Getting Your
Financial and Legal Life in Order*

You are pregnant. With an actual person (possibly more than one person if you are ambitious). I think this officially means you are an adult. I know, it's a lot. Being an adult means being responsible, which is kind of a buzzkill, but it's time. Your future child is counting on you. Beyond the obvious adulting requirements (a home, a job, an Amazon Prime membership) there are a few other tasks you should think about before baby arrives.

46. Make a Will

This seems like a bummer of a to-do item, but it's an important one. Get your will in order, including how your assets and child custody will be handled in the event of your death. It's a quick process that will ease your mind down the road. Visit info.legalzoom.com for more info on writing wills.

47. Get Life Insurance

This is another big adult activity and one that often gets overlooked. Life insurance is not that expensive, and it can provide security for your family. Research whole vs. term life insurance and decide which one is best for your budget and needs. Sign up, make your monthly payment, and put it out of your mind.

48. START RESEARCHING COLLEGE SAVINGS PLANS

This might seem a little premature, but there are a lot of options when it comes to saving for your child's future. Trust me when I tell you that researching these options will be a difficult task once you are in full parenting mode (full parenting mode mostly involves just surviving each day, not so much thinking about 18 years down the line). U.S. citizens can visit Savingforcollege.com for a ton of information on various college savings options. Canadians can visit Canada.ca to begin their research into college savings plans supported by the government. Feel free to also talk to a financial planner, but be aware that broker-sold plans often come with higher prices and fees.

CHAPTER 13

MAXIMIZE THE FUN

Tips for Fun Things to Do with Friends Before Your Free Time Becomes a Little Less Free

Wild nights with your friends may be a thing of the past now that you are pregnant, but that doesn't mean you can't still have a little fun. A lot of attention is paid to babymoons and maximizing time with your partner, but I think you should also take the time to connect with your friends during pregnancy. As all of our lives get busy with family and jobs it can become increasingly difficult to get time on the books with your closest girlfriends. Make those dates now, before your time gets even more limited.

49. Say Yes To a Girls' Night Out

You are pregnant and tired, so a girls' night out might only include you eating a meal and chatting with friends for a few hours. That's fine, go with it. If someone invites you out for drinks after work, say yes (and have a Shirley Temple). If your friends beg you to join them for a birthday party, begrudgingly show up, even if you'd rather be napping. Finding time to be social can be a difficult task once you have a baby, so use your pregnancy months to stock up on friend time before you go into a bit of a hibernation (a unique hibernation that involves no actual sleep).

50. Plan a Girls' Night In

You don't have to go big to have fun; staying home can be just as useful for connecting with friends during your pregnancy months. Invite a few friends over for appetizers and wine (water for you) and soak in some solid bonding from the comfort of your own home. Tell everyone it's a pajama party and you'll have the makings of the best pregnancy party ever.

51. Fight Through the Tired

I know you are tired, I know you feel bloated, I know you'd rather eat ice cream on the couch than put on real shoes and go out into the real world for the sake of socialization. But fight through all those relaxation instincts and force yourself to go have a little fun every once in awhile. You'll always be happy you did once you are out, and you'll miss these get-togethers later on.

Chapter 14

Babymoon

Where, When, and How to "Moon"

Babymoons are kind of like honeymoons, but instead of marking the beginning of a marriage they exist to remind you of the impending end of the life you're used to. So, you know, super festive. This chapter offers some tips on how to maximize your final good ol' days.

Keep in mind that the best time for pregnancy travel is during your second trimester. You're (hopefully) past your morning sickness phase and not yet into the completely exhausted days of the third trimester. Wherever you go be sure to pack essentials like comfy clothes, easily accessible healthy snacks, and any items you have that help you get a good night's sleep.

Take frequent walk/stretch breaks while traveling long distances to keep blood circulating, and try not to travel more than 5–6 hours at a time. Also, clear all travel plans with your doctor before you head out on your babymoon adventure.

52. GO BiG

Plan a big, fantastic trip into the lap of luxury because luxury is not a lap you are going to be visiting for quite a while post-baby. Maybe head to an all-inclusive resort or rent a beachfront house for a week. Yes, it will be expensive, but you're worth it!

53. GO SMall

Your babymoon doesn't have to be extravagant to be fun and memorable. Even a weekend away at a nearby hotel can meet the required activities (see sidebar) for your babymoon experience. The point is to get away and spend some one-on-one time with your partner before baby—beyond that there isn't a spending requirement attached to the trip.

54. JUST GO

Babymoons don't have to be intricately planned experiences either. One of the great joys of pre-parenthood life is your ability to do whatever the hell you want, whenever the hell you want. Take advantage of this freedom and decide to do something spontaneous a few times throughout your pregnancy. Day trip to a local lake or park. Hop in the car after work on Friday and drive until you get somewhere interesting. Buy last-minute theater tickets and head into the city for a date night. Be free!

55. OR STAY

Maybe you aren't up for anything other than lounging around the house in your pajamas watching crappy reality shows and ordering takeout. That sounds like a vacation to me! And you can still meet all your babymoon checklist requirements! Cheap and productive!

EXTRA: MANDATORY BABYMOON CHECKLIST

- ☐ Napping
- ☐ Sex
- ☐ Eating good food
- ☐ Conversation

Chapter 15

Baby Spaces

Tips on How to Get the House Pretty and Ready for Baby

A lot of time the nursery gets all of the attention when it comes to preparing the house for a new baby. But let's be honest, this child is going to take over every square inch of your home, not just one adorably designed room. Here are some ways to get all of your square footage baby-ready.

56. Decorate The Nursery

Some people get the nursery ready months in advance, and some people don't even order their crib until after the baby has made it home. I'd recommend landing somewhere between those two extremes so that you have enough time to assemble the room to your liking and also aren't picking out nursery items in a newborn panic.

Use your Nursery Pinterest board to collect nursery ideas and narrow down what elements you want to include. Keep in mind that the baby is going to weigh less than 10 pounds and be in blob form for a couple of months upon arrival. Which is to say, they don't have a lot of needs when it comes to extravagant room design.

I recommend getting the basics: crib, changing table, diaper pail, dresser, and a really comfy rocking chair that also reclines. The really comfy reclining rocking chair most likely won't win you any design awards, but it will become your bestest friend during middle-of-the-night and all-day feedings. Trust me.

51. ORGANIZE THE LIVING ROOM

You will find that one of the biggest changes in your life post-baby is the fact that you now spend most of your time on the floor. As babies get older the floor becomes a great place for them to do tummy time, learn to crawl, and play with toys. And there you will be, on the floor, tummy timing right along with them. Because of this fact I recommend getting your carpets cleaned or purchasing a nice fluffy new rug to prepare for your upcoming change in elevation.

I also recommend getting a couple medium-sized baskets and putting them in the living room. Babies come with a lot of accessories and toys, and somehow all those accessories and toys will end up in the middle of your living room on a daily basis. No one knows how this happens, but those baskets will provide a handy storage spot for the accessories and also give you quick access when they all need to be dumped on to the floor once again.

The living room is a great place for other baby items such as a rock-and-play, a swing, a playmat, nursing pillows, and a changing pad. Isn't it cute that you thought your baby would take up only one room of your house?

58. PREPARE THE KITCHEN

Granted, the baby is probably not going to be doing much cooking right away, but you'd be surprised at how they are still able to take over this space. The kitchen sink is a great place to bathe the baby when they are brand new. Put the baby bath in the sink and voilà, it's a little baby spa area that is convenient and comfortable for both of you.

The counters will also need to be lined with bottles and bottle drying racks so make sure you stock up on both.

59. ORGANIZE YOUR OFFICE

These days more and more people are doing some or all of their jobs from home. This means that you will often have an office set up in your house. Periodically you may need to bring the baby into your office while you tend to some work matters. Prepare for these visits by making room to drag the swing and rock-and-play from the living room into this area.

A basket of toys is a good idea in this room as well because quick entertainment is necessary when trying to deal with a work emergency while holding a disgruntled baby.

60. Add to YOUR ROOM

Personally, both of my kids slept in my room for months after we got home. Their nurseries were adorable but not visited much right away. If you want your baby near you, there are various bassinet and co-sleeping cots that can be set up right next to the side of your bed for easy access and/or overbearing monitoring.

61. DON'T FORGET OUTSIDE

Both of my kids absolutely loved being outside when they were teeny tiny babies. A trip to the backyard or front yard was often the only surefire way to calm down a crying fit. Get your backyard or patio prepared for baby by purchasing a comfortable glider chair for outdoor rocking. Also get a compact baby rocker that will allow the baby to lounge in the great outdoors and stare up at the sky and trees.

62. Baby-Proof The Whole House

Keep in mind that baby-proofing is not something you will need to do right away, since your baby will be immobile for quite awhile. But it's always a good idea to get a jump on anything that might take a lot of effort to complete once the baby is already here. You probably aren't going to have the energy to install outlet covers and baby locks throughout the house when the child is six months old, so you might as well tackle the task before you are battling sleep deprivation and an increasingly mobile child.

Chapter 16

Baby Prep

Get Educated Before Baby Arrives

One of the craziest things you will ever experience is the fact that you will be allowed to simply leave a hospital with your newborn baby shortly after giving birth. No one will seem to care that you are completely unqualified for this job or responsibility. Meanwhile your ineptitude will be all you can think about. How are you going to take care of a baby?! Who thought this was a good idea?? And why did you receive more instruction on how to parallel park your car than you ever received on how to care for a newborn? This can't be good. Especially considering how bad you are at parallel parking.

First of all, breathe. You got this. Second of all, it doesn't hurt to do a little studying before your baby gets here so that you can at least pretend to know what you are doing.

63. Find Classes and Books About Babies

There are roughly 78,695,834,207 classes and books available for you to learn everything you could possibly want to know about babies before you are in possession of your own. I tend to think that your baby itself will be your best teacher, but if you are looking for something a little less trial-by-fire there is no shortage of information available.

Books and internet articles are always a good place to start when researching any questions you may have, so put down the pregnancy books occasionally and hop over to the baby books to get a glimpse of your coming attractions.

While reading is a good educational warm-up, in-person classes will provide you with the opportunity to ask questions and get personalized advice from a real instructor. Often these classes will offer you a tiny baby doll on which to practice your skills, which is just like real life, if your baby never cried or moved.

The most important skill I ever learned in a baby class was infant CPR and how to assist a choking baby. Both of my babies were apparently very lazy chewers, and I used the choking assist more times than I can count. Find a way to learn this skill because it will come in very, very handy.

I will also mention that once you have the baby you will have a day or two to absorb as much knowledge as you can from your nurses and doctors before you leave the hospital. Personally I treated this time as Baby Bootcamp. I asked my nurses 35 questions an hour and had them repeatedly demonstrate every necessary baby maneuver I needed to know. I recommend you do the same.

64. VISIT FRIENDS WITH BABIES

If you have friends with real live babies, see if they will allow you to visit and take notes. Maybe you could even practice some of your classroom skills on something non-plastic. Keep in mind that every baby is different and you will develop your own strategies in how to best parent your own, so don't beat yourself up if you aren't completely in tune with your friend's baby upon first meeting.

65. GeT The CaR SeaT iN The CaR

This seems like a pretty basic task, but a lot of people put it off until after the baby arrives. Get your car seat base in your car and have it inspected by a certified car seat technician. You can usually find these technicians in your area by searching for "Car Seat Safety Checks" along with your city's name.

66. HOPe FOR The BeST

Let's be honest, no matter how many books you read or how many classes you take, there is nothing that will totally prepare you for the crazy, wonderful, overwhelming experience of bringing home your first baby. Try to not panic too much about all the things you don't know. You'll figure them out, just like every other parent who has ever been completely terrified by a tiny little human. Before long, you will be the one getting the texts from the frazzled new moms looking for advice. It's the circle of parenting life, really. First the frazzled student, then the frazzled teacher.

EXTRA:
Skills to Learn Before Baby

- ☐ Infant CPR/How to Help a Choking Baby
- ☐ How to Change a Diaper
- ☐ Swaddling a Baby
- ☐ Latching Tips
- ☐ How to Do Every Major Life Necessity with a Baby Hanging Off Your Boob

Chapter 17

Maternity Photos

More Than Just the Fancy Photos

Pregnancy can have a way of making you feel less than photogenic. You're tired, everything is bloated, and the last thing you want to do is document this unfortunate combination. But trust me when I tell you that 1) someday you'll wish you took a million photos of the time you spent growing your baby from scratch and 2) someday you'll marvel at how good you looked, even in your tired, puffy state. So don't run away from the camera, embrace it!

67. TAKE THE PHOTOS!

When in doubt, take a picture. This generation of children will be the first to have nearly every day of their lives documented via their parents' phones, so you might as well start the story from the very beginning. Your goal is to be able to flip through the photos from your pregnancy months and have an animation of sorts where your belly gets bigger and bigger in service of the coolest science experiment ever.

Candid photos and quick snapshots are a great way to capture this time. Also make a point to take monthly photos, preferably in the same location, to chronical your expanding belly.

For a more professional look research maternity photographers in your area and book a photoshoot for your third trimester. I know you feel huge, but you are beautiful and this is a moment you want captured. Also, professional photographers can offer great lighting and editing skills, which is always a nice combo when you are hoping for a good shot.

68. STEAL IDEAS FROM THE INTERNET

The internet is jam-packed with maternity photo ideas that other people executed to perfection. They run the gamut from the adorable incorporation of the baby's name to the odd submersion in a bathtub full of milk. If you are looking for traditional ideas, artistic ideas, or ideas that involve you getting naked in a field, the internet is here to provide you with various ways to make your vision a reality. Scour all of these photos and pick out the ones you like the best. Then take some similar ones or send them to your professional photographer so she knows what shots you are hoping to get.

69. Fill The FRaMe

Don't forget to include your friends, family, and partner or spouse in your photos throughout your pregnancy. You'll love having photo proof of those who took this journey with you. On the day of your professional photoshoot make sure to include your partner for added adorableness. In addition, consider inviting your parents or grandparents for a few photos as well. Documenting your family's generations will be a photo you will cherish forever (but maybe don't involve any of these people if you decide to go the milk-bath maternity photo route).

70. GeT Videos, Too

Don't forget about moving pictures as well. Videos are a great way to really capture who you were while you were pregnant. Take videos of yourself solo, with your partner, and with your family members. Talk to the baby about how excited you are to meet them, all the plans you have for their little life, and how completely terrified you are of their upcoming arrival. Kids will love watching these videos when they are older.

Chapter 18

YOUR SUPPORT NETWORK

People You Can Count on During
and After Pregnancy

Pregnancy and parenting aren't easy. The good news is, you don't have to go through either alone. We live in a digital world, full of social media, texting, and constant connection via various electronic devices. This is great news for pregnant woman and moms. It means that answers, a sympathetic ear, and camaraderie are always within arm's reach. And trust me, you are going to need all of those and more once you find yourself responsible for the well-being of a new baby.

Start building up your support network now so that they are ready to connect when you need it most.

71. FiNd The MaMaS

Doctors and the internet will provide you with a great deal of guidance during your first days/months/years with a new baby, but nothing can compare to the advice offered by "been there, seen way too much of that" moms. Find as many moms as you can, and hold them close. Offer your support and humor when they need it, and don't hesitate to reach out when you are struggling as well. Trust me when I tell you that you will be welcomed with open arms into the Mom Club and you will value its members more than you could ever imagine.

72. Reach OuT To YouR MaMa

Often a shift happens when you have kids of your own, wherein you suddenly start to understand your own mother in a way you weren't able to before you brought a baby home. Depending on your relationship with your mom, this can bring up a lot of different emotions. But if you are lucky enough to have a good relationship with your mom and have her in your life she can become an excellent source of support pre- and post-baby.

13.
Build your digital support group

Start building a list of moms and friends in your life that won't hesitate to answer your frantic baby texts all hours of the day and night. Texting will become your primary mode of communication post-baby, and you need to know which of your contacts are professionals in the texting department. Who responds quickly, who has the best sense of humor, who has all the answers, who sends the best emojis? These are important questions.

Also, look for and join mom groups on social media. These groups are often private and provide a sense of community during those very isolating baby days. Find wide-ranging groups as well as groups of local moms—you might even find a playdate partner or two in the mix.

Chapter 19

Baby Shower

How to Have the Perfect Baby Party

Baby showers are a rite of passage for pregnant ladies. It is rule that friends and family must shower the expectant mother with baby whatnots while eating finger sandwiches and mini quiches. Some women are giddy at the thought of having a baby shower, and others are less than thrilled to endure the hours-long pastel and onesie explosion. Wherever you land on the scale try to embrace the shower and figure out a way to make it your own.

74. Be Vocal

If a friend has offered to plan and host your shower make sure you let her know any strong opinions you have in regard to your special day. Some friends mean well but end up planning the kind of shower they would want instead of asking you what you want.

In my case I didn't have too many strong shower opinions, other than the fact that I was really opposed to games. I let it be known that no one would be smelling diapers or measuring bellies or stealing clothes pins. It's important to stand up for what you believe in.

Sit down with your shower hostess early on in the process and hammer out the details that are important to you. She wants to throw you a great party, so her feelings will not be hurt if you tell her the kind of party you want it to be.

75. Be Cheap

There's no reason to break the bank on a baby shower. Your friends and family want to come celebrate you and your baby—they won't care if the event is not catered and brimming with expensive flowers and favors. Have the party at a private residence to avoid the fees associated with renting a space. Send digital invitations instead of paper ones. Food can be simple appetizers and can be delegated to a few willing friends who want to help out. Homemade cookies in a cute little bag make great party favors. Games can be limited to easy/

cheap options (quizzes; blank advice cards for filling out; have everyone bring a baby photo and try to match the guests to their younger selves).

Keep it simple—the day is about celebrating you and your baby, not extravagance.

16. Go Co-ed

Co-ed showers are a new trend and are essentially just a party with some onesies thrown in. Which sounds like a good time to me. This is a great chance for your partner to feel connected to your pregnancy and an all-around fun way to tackle your baby shower requirement. You can still hit the shower basics but switch them up a bit for a co-ed audience (think BBQ, beer, and inappropriate shower games).

17. The More The Easier

I think we ended up having four baby showers for our firstborn. This sounds excessive, but it was really nice. If you're like me you might have a lot of different groups of friends. Work friends, childhood friends, family, etc. Having all those people in one place for one big baby shower can be a little overwhelming and a rather large party to plan.

Instead, consider having a few showers with smaller groups. The smaller groups will give you a chance to actually chat with the people who come to shower your baby and might not be as stressful as one huge shower.

CHAPTER 20

PARTY OF TWO

Fun Stuff to Do with Your Partner While You Are Still Only a Party of Two

Pregnancy is an exciting time for a couple. It marks the bridge between partnership and full-blown family unit. It also marks the last days of calm before the storm hits. Take advantage of these last days when it's just the two of you. Have fun, get to know each other again, go on a few adventures, and always, always nap as much as humanly possible because the storm is going to be an exhausting one.

18. Talk!

Once you have kids you will find that normal adult conversations take a bit of a hiatus from your household. You and your partner are both tired, overwhelmed by new parenthood, and frankly don't have much to talk about besides diaper blowouts and nipple guards.

Maximize your pre-baby days by talking as much as possible. It may seems silly, but undivided attention will be in short supply once you become a party of three. Offer it up to each other as much as you can during these pregnancy months.

After the baby arrives try to keep these conversations going, even if it's only once a day. Take the time to connect and try to talk about something other than the screaming child.

79. Date Your Partner

Even after you have kids it's really important to keep dating your spouse (it might be even more important after you have kids). So get in the habit now of setting dates with each other. Plan a night out for dinner and a movie. Or maybe go catch a game if you have a professional sports team in the area. Put the dates on your calendar and stick with them, even if you are feeling a little tired.

80. Do Nothing at All

One of the things I miss most about life pre-kids is my ability to spend my nights and weekends doing ABSOLUTELY NOTHING if I wanted to. I could plop on the couch and watch movies, or go to bed early, or sleep in late, or stare at a wall all day if I wanted to (because I've always been a party animal). Pregnancy marks your last months of freedom, but freedom doesn't need to be exploited by taking constant adventures. Sometimes the freedom to exert no energy whatsoever is the greatest freedom at all. Bask in it together.

81. BE INDEPENDENT

This may sound like a weird tip, but I think it's important. Before you have kids, even if you are married, even if you are living together, even if you share a life, the fact is, you are still pretty independent. Your partner won't be affected much if you have to work late, or want to go catch coffee with a friend, or spend the day curled up with a book and solitude.

All this comes to an end once you are sharing the responsibility of caring for a baby. Once you have a baby, activities like working late, or coffee with a friend, or reading in solitude mean that you will be leaving your partner to care for a child, and that will leave you feeling guilty.

Take advantage of this time before the guilt sets in. Allow each other a little freedom to be independent, knowing that come Baby Time both of you are fully committed to showing up for duty.

Chapter 21

Career

Preparing Your Career for Hurricane Baby

You are woman, hear you roar. Or at least, hear you plan. If you will be working after you have your baby there are a lot of different issues for you to consider well before your due date. I'm a firm believer in women tearing up the workplace and showing their children what it means to work hard and provide for their family. But I also know, from a lot of experience, that it's very difficult to balance work and parenthood. Often the balance leaves moms feeling as if they aren't doing justice to work or their kid. Understand that you are not alone if you find yourself struggling as a working parent, and come up with a solid plan as to how you are going to tackle this huge undertaking post-baby.

82. PLAN MATERNITY LEAVE

Maternity leave is such an important time for you and your baby. In Canada, the government offers maternity leave up to 18 months for both parents, with a portion of their salary covered through a government program. This is a huge amount of maternity leave, which is nice, but it still leaves a gap in income.

In the U.S. if you have worked at your job for more than a year and you work more than 25 hours a week, you are entitled, by law, to 12 weeks of maternity leave (dads are eligible for paternity leave as well). Your position must be held for you during that time, which is great news. The bad news is that your company is not required to pay you during that time, so you need to make sure you plan well in advance for the financial reality of your time off. Vacation and sick time can be combined to keep your paycheck coming while you are off so start stockpiling both long before you are even pregnant. If those are not an available option look into the paid disability leave offered by your state. Short-term disability insurance policies can also be a good way to bring in some money during your maternity leave.

Plan in advance for the financial aspects of maternity leave so that you can enjoy your time with your new baby without having to be stressed out about being able to pay the bills.

83. Make a Back-to-Work Plan

Getting back to work after maternity leave can be a bit of an adjustment. Even if you are able to take a long time off you will still be heading into the office with the exhaustion of new motherhood every day. Take this into consideration when planning your return to the office. If possible, try to start out part-time, to ease yourself back into the day-to-day requirements of work. Also maybe try to fit a pillow and blanket under your desk for midday napping breaks.

Discuss your back-to-work transition with your partner and make sure you are both on the same page about sharing the baby load 50/50. This will not only help lighten the load but will also stave off any festering resentment from a partner who is feeling overextended and not adequately supported with household duties. Resentment has a way of becoming unfestered around 3:00 a.m., via very quiet (Don't wake the baby!), but very animated arguments—so do your best to avoid this if at all possible.

84. Make a Childcare Plan

As a working parent, quality childcare will become your number one concern. Leaving your baby will be extremely difficult, especially at the beginning. Having a childcare provider you trust will give you priceless peace of mind while you are at work. Childcare options can vary from nannies, to nanny-sharing, in-home day care, and larger day care facilities. Explore all these options and talk with other moms to figure out what sounds like the best fit for you. Then visit and interview and take your time finding just the right childcare provider for your baby.

85. ACKNOWLEDGE WORK LIMITATIONS

Again, you are woman, and you will roar. You can work and be a mom and have it ALL! But you also need to be realistic about what restrictions a baby is going to put on your professional life. Is your job conducive to the demands that a baby will have on your time? Is there a way to alter your job requirements (even temporarily) to give you the best chance of succeeding at work and at home?

Thinking about this before your baby arrives will help you be realistic in planning for your life once it has a baby bouncing around in it.

Chapter 22

Fur Babies

Helping Your Pets Get Ready for Baby

Fur babies are often part of our lives before human babies come on the scene. Just like the rest of the family, your pets are going to have a rude awakening once hurricane baby comes swirling through the house. Help them, and yourself, by considering your animals when planning for the hurricane's arrival.

86. PLAN SOME DRY RUNS

If you have friends with kids see if you can meet up for a playdate where your pet can come face-to-face with a real-life little person. It's a good idea to see how your pet reacts to children and plan for any behavior issues that might become a problem.

87. STOCK UP

Does your pet need special medicine, food, or other supplies? Stock up on all things animal before the baby comes so that it's one less thing you have to worry about once you enter your newborn haze.

88. SET UP a PET SITTER

When planning for your delivery and post-baby hospital stay make sure you line up a pet sitter to take care of Fido or Kitty during your absence. In the case of Fido it can also be nice to have a pet sitter keep your dog(s) for a couple days after you get back home with the baby, just to give you a minute to settle in without worrying about feeding/walking the dog.

89. TEACH GENTLE HANDS

Babies and little kids can be rough with pets, and often pets put up with it. But remember that your fur babies are more fur than they are baby and it's always a good idea to teach your kids about kindness to animals from Day 1. Your own animals may be patient with a baby/toddler climbing on them or occasionally pulling a tail, but your child might not be so lucky when they come across other animals outside of your home.

Teach your children that pets are animals first and to always proceed with caution and kindness when interacting with them. This will educate them on how to be safe and respectful around other animals they come into contact with throughout their youth.

CHaPTeR 23

BiRTh PLaN

What to Consider When Trying to Plan Something That Is Completely Beyond Your Control

The concept of a birth plan is hilarious to me because I've found that babies have their own plans and don't really care much about anything you might have in mind. But it's never a bad idea to get some basic preferences down on paper and take the time to really think about what you want as far as your delivery is concerned.

Instead of starting from scratch I recommend finding a birth plan template to work with. Sites like Mybirthplan.com and Freebirthplan.com offer comprehensive birth plan templates that are easy to fill out and print before the big day.

90. DO YOUR RESEARCH

A lot of women have pretty set ideas about what they want in regard to their childbirthing experience. They know if they want to be at home or a hospital or a birthing center. They know if they want to go all natural or involve an epidural. They know if they want a doula. They know if they want a birthing ball, swimming pool, and mirrors. But it still doesn't hurt to do a little research into all the options available for birthing. You never know what fun things you might have overlooked (because navigating a watermelon out of your uterus is a situation ripe with fun).

Read books, ask your doctor, quiz your friends with kids. If something strikes your interest dig a little deeper into what it takes to make it a reality for you and your baby. I do caution you, however, that any research into birth plans can result in a lot of horror stories that may leave you deeply traumatized. Proceed with caution and try to walk away instead of going down a birth story internet rabbit hole that will lead to nowhere fun.

91. PREPARE

If you want a doula, research and pick one early on. If you want music, make a playlist in your second trimester. If you want a birthing ball or a pool, get them ordered. Don't put off anything that can be done early. Having everything in place will ease your mind and won't leave you scrambling the last few weeks before your due date.

92. Share Your Birth Plan

Make sure your partner, doctor, and any other important players are made aware of your birth plan and preferences. A lot of the time it will be up to these individuals to try to make sure things go the way you want them to. If something is really, really important to you, be vocal about it and encourage your partner to fight for it on Baby Day.

93. LET IT GO

After you plan and purchase and prepare and ponder, it's time to...let it go. You've put everything down on paper, you've made your wishes known to those around you, and you've set everything up for the birth of your dreams. That is all you can do. Now it's time to take a deep breath and come to peace with the fact that there is a chance that absolutely nothing on your birth plan will go as you planned. And that's okay.

The only real goal of childbirth is the birth of your child. Keep that in mind if things start going off track at any point during your delivery. You can't control how your child comes into this world—it's just your job to be there to catch them and hold them tight once they make their big entrance.

Chapter 24

After-Birth Plan

Tips on Putting Together a General Plan for How Things Will Go Once You Get the Baby Home

I happen to be of the general mindset that having an after-birth plan is just as, if not more, important than your birth plan. Because even if you don't have a birth plan, you'll still be giving birth, and you'll probably be surrounded by medical professionals who know how to handle such things. Unfortunately, those medical professionals do not come home with you to help you take care of your baby after your birth (trust me, I asked if they would).

When you get home with a new baby you'll be tired, overwhelmed, and dealing with whack-a-doodle hormone changes. Do as much as you can now to plan for those early days so you can spend your time focusing on your new baby, instead of all these little details.

94. Plan on Visitors

Try to decide in advance if you want visitors (and which visitors you want) to come to the hospital or your home after the baby arrives. Make a list of the visitors you'd like to see and share that list with your partner. It will then be your partner's responsibility to enforce that list. Alert the enforcer that you may completely change your mind about visitors after the baby is born so make sure all visits are tentative until you give the thumbs-up.

Sometimes family or cultural customs make it difficult to enforce a strict visitor policy post-baby. In that case, make sure you and your partner at least devise hand signals and/or a secret code language so that you can slyly let it be known when you've reached your visitor limit. It will be your partner's job to act as your buffer and hopefully keep visitors in line if you are feeling overwhelmed.

95. Set Up a Meal/Visit Calendar

If you have friends and family who want to help out with a meal once you get home with the baby it might be a good idea to set up an account with a website like Mealbaby.com or Mealtrain.com to assist with the coordination of the meals/visits when the time comes. These sites offer easy and convenient registering and scheduling, and anything that is easy and convenient is worth making a part of your life.

96. ACCEPT THAT BREASTFEEDING IS HARD

This isn't so much a tip as it is a warning. Breastfeeding has been billed as the best and most natural choice when it comes to feeding your baby. Moms go into breastfeeding expecting it to be easy because it's "natural." I would just like to point out that nature can be a bit of a pain.

Women can have all sorts of issues with breastfeeding—from a baby that won't latch, to milk that won't come in, to bleeding nipples. I'm not saying this to discourage you from breastfeeding but to give you a heads-up that it can be HARD. I feel like going into breastfeeding with the knowledge that it is hard can help you mentally prepare for the struggles. Don't quit just because it's hard—you aren't the only one struggling; difficulties are completely "natural" as well.

If your hospital offers lactation specialists request a consultation as soon as the baby pops out. There are also breastfeeding support groups online, and the La Leche League (llli.org) provides tons of resources and meet-ups for breastfeeding moms.

97. PREPARE FOR POSTPARTUM BLUES

Postpartum depression is talked about a lot, but it still comes as a bit of a surprise when it happens to you. Somehow women think that they will be immune to postpartum baby blues, as if they can just will their hormones to stay in line. But 80% of new moms experience some sort of postpartum emotional issue, ranging from "baby blues" to full-on postpartum depression. And yet, you will rarely hear a woman talk about her postpartum issues until well after she's recovered from them because even though we all know how common the issues are, we still feel shame when they happen to us.

As you are preparing for your life post-baby, make sure you are being honest with yourself about the possibility of postpartum depression. Confirm that you have an OB who will follow up about your mental health at every postpartum visit. If you've suffered from depression previously, line up a therapist that you can check in with after your baby arrives.

Postpartum depression can take on different forms. You may feel extremely sad for no reason or sometimes even manically happy. You may have bouts of anxiety or rage or hopelessness. These are all completely normal, but if you experience any of these let your doctor know immediately. Also have your partner and other friends and family keep an eye out for any of these symptoms. Vow to keep the conversation open once the baby arrives and make sure you are all on the lookout for any possible issues.

Postpartum blues and depression are completely treatable and in no way something that should be covered up. Keep telling yourself that throughout your pregnancy and you'll be ready to deal with these issues if they pop up post-baby.

98. AGREE ON DUTY SHARING

Parenthood is a team sport. And no one gets out of playing simply because they are a rookie. Sit down with your partner before the baby arrives and hammer out some details of your life as new parents. Get on the same page about how you will split up the baby and house duties once the newborn comes home. For example, if mama is planning to breastfeed then her partner can vow to take on most of the diaper changes or do the dishes and laundry that have an unexplained way of piling to the ceiling as soon as you bring a tiny baby home.

Have these duty-sharing conversations before the baby arrives because you'd be surprised how many couples are not on the same page about these matters. And it's not a great idea to discover this difference of opinion at 2:30 a.m. when both parents are sleep deprived and covered in spit-up. Trust me.

Chapter 25

Countdown to Baby

Things to Do Your Last Month Before Baby

You are in the homestretch. Your due date is mere weeks away. You are a majestic bird, getting ready to spread your wings into new parenthood. Unfortunately, you are also nine months pregnant and feel like a considerably less aerodynamic animal, perhaps of the beached whale variety.

The good news is that your bloated days are numbered; the bad news is that pretty soon you will be responsible for the survival of a tiny little person who comes with no instruction manual. Try not to freak out.

The tips in this chapter are important, but they also take into account your overall beached whale disposition. Do them slowly, preferably from the comfort of a couch or bed. Let them guide you as you waddle toward your pregnancy finish line.

99. LOAD YOUR PHONE WITH APPS

There are countless apps available to help you navigate parenthood. Some are geared specifically to baby days, while others will follow you through all of the childhood years. Use your well-rested brain to research these apps now because they will offer a lot of support when you need it most.

Also, add entertainment apps to your phone. Amazon Prime, Hulu, and Netflix offer phone apps, and most network and cable stations do as well. These apps will prove handy during late-night feedings with your baby. Turn on the closed captioning option to keep things quiet, and you can binge watch countless shows while your baby binge eats. Win-win.

If you like reading you may find that operating a real book becomes a bit cumbersome while holding a baby, so add a book-reading app (like Kindle) to your phone now and load it up with several different genres of books you want to read. Keep in mind that your sleep-deprived haze will probably make it difficult to comprehend anything too dense.

Basically your phone will become your lifeline in the first weeks and months of new parenthood, so jam it full of as many features as you can now.

100. Take LOTS of NaPS

It is not possible to adequately explain how much you will miss naps once your child has excised them from your life. Do yourself a favor and appreciate them while they are still available to you. Hold them close and do not waste any of your last days together.

101. PREP and FREEZE MeaIS

Sleep deprivation and newborn baby maintenance do not inspire a lot of cooking. But it turns out that eating is important, even if most of your meals will now be consumed while bouncing a baby on your hip. Get ahead of the game before the baby arrives. Prep some meals and freeze them for easy reheating post-baby. Also, stockpile local take-out menus because even the microwave might seem like too much effort during the first weeks of baby.

102. PACK FOR THE HOSPITAL

This seems like a pretty basic to-do item, but you would be surprised how many people don't get around to packing their hospital bag. This can result in the frantic throwing of 8,924 household items into a grocery bag as soon as contractions start. Don't be the person who brings a toaster to the delivery room. Plan, and pack, ahead.

✓ EXTRA: What to Pack for the Hospital

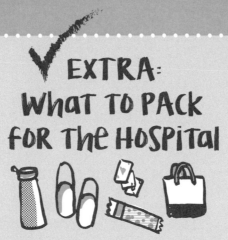

- ☐ Comfy birthing outfit
- ☐ Slippers
- ☐ Playing cards/magazines for passing the time if baby is in no hurry
- ☐ 10 onesies for the baby
- ☐ Snacks for a long delivery and to supplement horrible hospital food post-delivery
- ☐ An extra bag to fill with free hospital loot
- ☐ Treat/gift for the nurses
- ☐ Three nannies
- ☐ Other Notes: _____

_____

_____

_____

_____

_____

EPilogue: Baby Days

This book is called 102 Things to Do Before You Are Due, but I don't want to abandon you at the finish line of pregnancy. We've come this far together, and I can't leave without giving you a few final thoughts to take with you into your first weeks with your new baby.

My experience with my second baby was so much different than the one I had with my first. Everything just felt a little easier the second time around. But when I think about it, my two babies weren't that much different from each other. So, what got easier? What changed?

Upon closer inspection it's clear that my babies might not have been different, but I was a completely different person the second time around.

When I brought my first baby home I was overwhelmed by all the things I didn't know and by all the ways I wasn't perfect. Now that I'm years into this parenting game, it seems absolutely ridiculous that I ever thought perfection was a possibility. But at the very beginning I held tight to my delusion.

Back then I was used to being good at things, and if I wasn't good at something I was used to being able to put in the work to figure out how to master the task at hand. But this new baby threw me for a loop. I had no idea what I was doing, and every time I thought I was getting a handle on any part of parenting, every part would change. What worked one day to calm the baby would be completely useless 24 hours later. Time seemed to be moving in slow motion, which was still faster than my tired brain was operating. And worst of all, I felt like I was most definitely the only woman who had ever been this bad at parenting.

So before I leave you, I want to share one last tip. The most important one of all.

MASTER TIP:
BE GENTLE
WITH YOURSELF

My second baby wasn't easier, I was easier. I was easier on him and on myself. I had managed to keep his sister alive, so my first days with him weren't weighed down with never-ending uncertainty about my abilities. I knew he was going to cry and not sleep, and I was going to cry and not sleep, and we would both eventually stop crying and maybe even sleep a little (my expectations for the second kid were set a little lower than the first).

I knew breastfeeding was going to be difficult, so I wasn't shocked when my nipples almost fell off. I knew that I was going to have some postpartum depression issues, so I didn't try to hide or ignore them. I knew it was all going to be so, so hard, but I also knew that it would eventually get better, so I didn't let myself get buried in the temporary struggles. Somehow knowing all these things made the second time around a little easier.

I know that nothing I say will magically transform every new mom into a ball of confidence and optimism. But I hope that at the very least you will hold on tight to this last tip. In your first few days, weeks, and months of new parenthood, always try to remember to be gentle with yourself. You might not know what you are doing, you might be drowning in hormones and sleep deprivation, you might have had a pretty heated argument with your breast pump yesterday. But you are going to be okay. I promise.

Take a deep breath, make peace with the breast pump, and

tackle today with all you've got. Hand the baby to your partner or to a friend and take a shower or a nap (or a nap in the shower?). Throw on some sweats and some sunglasses and go for a walk around the block. Let go of any aspirations of perfection. Your baby doesn't need perfect. And quite frankly, your baby doesn't really have anyone else to compare you to, so you are pretty perfect to them.

Be gentle with yourself, and your new baby, in the beginning. Give each of you some time to settle into your new lives. Like every other parent on the planet, you'll figure it out. You'll get to know this new little person, and they will get to know you.

If you are feeling sad or manic or angry or anxiety-ridden, don't push those feelings down. Share them with your partner and your doctor so that you can all come up with a plan to help. Postpartum issues are very common and nothing to be ashamed of. Be gentle with yourself and seek out help when you need it.

And then continue to be gentle with yourself even after the newborn haze wears off. And be gentle with other parents you meet along the way. This motherhood journey isn't an easy one, but traveling it with other parents will make the road a little more enjoyable.

And always, always remember, you grew this little person from a tiny speck into a real live being, then you navigated that being out of your body and into this world. That's pretty badass. There's nothing this child can offer up that you can't handle. You MAKE PEOPLE in your spare time, so you can manage a little crying and spit-up (okay, a lot of crying and spit-up).

You got this, mama.

Index

Library of Congress Cataloging-in-Publication Data available upon request.

ISBN: 978-1-947458-49-9

Illustrated by Leticia Plate
Design by Kelley Lanuto, Kalanuto Design

duopress books are available at special discounts when purchased in bulk for sales promotions as well as for fund-raising or educational use. Special editions can be created to specification.
Contact us at hello@duopressbooks.com for more information.

Manufactured in China
10 9 8 7 6 5 4 3 2 1

Duopress LLC
8 Market Place, Suite 300
Baltimore, MD 21202

Distributed by Workman Publishing Company, Inc.
Published simultaneously in Canada by Thomas Allen & Son Limited.

To order: hello@duopressbooks.com
www.punchlineideas.com
www.duopressbooks.com
www.workman.com

ALSO FROM DUOPRESS

The Belly Sticker Book
ISBN: 9781946064998

The PREGNANCY BELLY
STICKER BOOK
ISBN: 9781947458444

Available everywhere!